AI in Leadership:

NAVIGATING THE FUTURE

authorHOUSE·

AuthorHouse™
1663 Liberty Drive
Bloomington, IN 47403
www.authorhouse.com
Phone: 833-262-8899

Published by AuthorHouse 02/20/2024

ISBN: 979-8-8230-2230-9 (sc)
ISBN: 979-8-8230-2229-3 (e)

Library of Congress Control Number: 2024903340

Print information available on the last page.

Contents

Abstract

Artificial intelligence (AI) stands as a transformative force reshaping industries, economies, and societies worldwide. This book aims to provide a comprehensive overview of AI, elucidating its definition, historical evolution, and the profound impact it has on modern civilization. By examining AI's inception, development, and current state, this book navigates the landscape of AI, unraveling its significance and future trajectory.

Introduction

Chapter 1

The AI Revolution Understanding AI

Understanding AI: Definition and Evolution

Artificial intelligence (AI) stands as a revolutionary field of computer science aimed at creating machines capable of performing tasks that typically require human intelligence. This comprehensive overview encompasses the various facets of AI, including its definition, subfields, applications, challenges, and future directions.

Definition of AI

AI refers to the simulation of human intelligence in machines programmed to think, learn, and execute tasks that traditionally have necessitated human cognitive abilities. It involves the development of algorithms that enable machines to perceive, reason, learn from data, and make decisions.

Subfields of AI

- Machine learning (ML): A subset of AI that empowers systems to automatically learn and improve from experience without explicit programming. ML algorithms include supervised learning, unsupervised learning, and reinforcement learning.
- Deep learning: A type of ML utilizing neural networks with multiple layers to model complex patterns in large datasets. Deep learning excels in image and speech recognition, natural language processing, and autonomous vehicles.
- Natural language processing (NLP): AI techniques enabling computers to understand, interpret, and generate human language.

Applications range from language translation and sentiment analysis to chatbots and language generation.
- Computer vision employs AI to interpret and process visual information from images or videos. Computer vision finds applications in facial recognition, object detection, medical imaging, and autonomous driving.

Applications of AI

AI's applications span various industries, including the following:

- health care: diagnosis assistance, drug discovery, personalized medicine
- finance: risk assessment, fraud detection, algorithmic trading
- manufacturing: predictive maintenance, quality control, supply chain optimization
- marketing: personalization, customer segmentation, recommendation systems
- transportation: autonomous vehicles, traffic management, route optimization

Challenges and Ethical Considerations

AI adoption presents challenges:

- ethical concerns: bias in algorithms, privacy violations, and job displacement
- regulatory challenges: establishing ethical guidelines and frameworks for AI governance
- data quality and bias: ensuring unbiased, high-quality data for training AI models

Future Trajectory

The future of AI holds numerous possibilities:

- explainable AI: developing models that provide transparent reasoning for their decisions

- ethical AI: prioritizing fairness, transparency, and accountability in AI systems
- AI in conjunction with other technologies: synergies with quantum computing, edge computing, and IoT

Conclusion

AI continues to evolve rapidly, reshaping industries and societies worldwide. Its potential to augment human capabilities, automate processes, and solve complex problems remains immense. However, as AI proliferates, addressing ethical concerns, ensuring accountability, and guiding its responsible development will be pivotal in harnessing its transformative power for the betterment of humanity.

Impact of AI on Business: Past, Present, and Future

The impact of AI on business spans across the past and present and holds profound implications for the future. Understanding this evolution illuminates the transformative power AI wields within the business landscape.

Past

- Emergence of AI in business: Historically, businesses have integrated AI to streamline processes, automate tasks, and enhance decision-making. Early AI applications focused on rule-based systems, aiding in simple automation tasks.
- Pioneering AI adoption: Early adopters in sectors like finance and manufacturing utilized AI for predictive modeling, fraud detection, and process optimization. However, limitations in computing power and data accessibility constrained widespread AI implementation.

Present

- AI-powered insights: Modern businesses leverage AI for advanced analytics, extracting actionable insights from vast datasets. This informs strategic decisions, customer targeting, and personalized marketing campaigns.
- Enhanced customer experience: AI-driven chatbots, recommendation systems, and personalized interactions revolutionize customer service, leading to higher satisfaction and engagement levels.
- Operational efficiency: Automation through AI streamlines operations, optimizing supply chains, inventory management, and production processes. Predictive maintenance reduces downtime and enhances productivity.

Future

- AI-driven innovation: Businesses are poised to witness an AI-driven innovation surge. Enhanced capabilities in machine learning and deep learning will spawn innovative products and services across industries.
- Industry disruption: AI's evolution is expected to disrupt traditional business models significantly. Sectors like health care, finance, and transportation will undergo radical transformations with AI-powered solutions.
- Ethical AI and governance: As AI proliferates, ensuring ethical AI development and robust governance frameworks will be critical. Striking a balance between innovation and ethical considerations will shape AI's future in business.

Challenges and Opportunities

- Skills and workforce: The need for AI-skilled professionals is rising. Businesses face the challenge of upskilling the workforce to harness AI's potential effectively.
- Data privacy and security: Addressing concerns regarding data privacy, security breaches, and the ethical use of consumer data remains a pressing challenge in AI integration.

Conclusion

The past and present illustrate AI's progressive integration into businesses, optimizing operations, enhancing decision-making, and transforming customer experiences. As businesses navigate the future, harnessing AI's potential while addressing ethical concerns and skill gaps will determine their competitive edge in an AI-driven marketplace. Embracing responsible AI adoption will not only drive innovation but also shape a sustainable and ethical future for businesses.

Why AI Matters in Today's Business Landscape

AI stands as a transformative force in today's business landscape due to its multifaceted impact, providing unprecedented opportunities and solutions that significantly influence business operations and success.

Data-Driven Decision-Making

- Insights from vast data: In an era flooded with data, AI's ability to analyze, interpret, and derive actionable insights from massive datasets enables informed decision-making. This empowers businesses to make strategic choices based on data-driven intelligence rather than intuition alone.

Operational Efficiency and Automation

- Process optimization: AI-driven automation streamlines workflows and optimizes processes, reducing operational costs and enhancing efficiency. Tasks that were once manual and time-consuming are now automated, freeing up resources for higher-value activities.

Enhanced Customer Experience

- Personalization and engagement: AI facilitates personalized customer experiences through recommendation systems, chatbots, and tailored marketing strategies. Understanding consumer behavior allows businesses to engage customers more effectively, leading to increased loyalty and satisfaction.

Innovation and Competitiveness

- Innovation catalyst: AI serves as a catalyst for innovation, enabling the development of new products, services, and business models. Businesses leveraging AI gain a competitive edge by fostering innovation and staying ahead in rapidly evolving markets.

Adaptability and Agility

- Agile responses: AI equips businesses with agility to adapt swiftly to market changes. Predictive analytics and AI-driven insights help anticipate trends and adapt strategies, allowing businesses to respond proactively to market shifts.

Scalability and Growth

- Scalable solutions: AI technologies provide scalable solutions that accommodate business growth. Automated systems and AI-driven processes scale more efficiently, catering to increased demands without proportional increases in resources.

Futureproofing and Sustainability

- Preparing for the future: Embracing AI today prepares businesses for the future. As AI technologies continue to advance, businesses that integrate AI early can remain adaptable and resilient in an evolving business landscape.

Conclusion

AI's significance in today's business landscape transcends mere technological adoption. It fundamentally alters business strategies, operational frameworks, and customer interactions. Embracing AI isn't just a competitive advantage; it's a necessity for businesses seeking sustainable growth, innovation, and relevance in an increasingly digital and data-centric world. Its integration shapes the foundation for future success and market leadership.

Foundations of AI in Business

Chapter 2

Fundamentals of AI

Exploring AI Concepts: Machine Learning, Deep Learning, Neural Networks

Machine Learning (ML)

Definition: Machine learning is a subset of AI that enables systems to learn and improve from experience without being explicitly programmed. It focuses on the development of algorithms allowing computers to learn patterns from data and make data-driven decisions.

- Types of Machine Learning
    - Supervised learning involves training a model on labeled data, enabling it to make predictions or decisions based on input-output pairs.
    - Unsupervised learning trains models on unlabeled data, allowing them to discover patterns and structures independently.
    - Reinforcement learning uses an agent interacting with an environment, learning to make sequences of decisions to maximize cumulative rewards.

- Applications
    - predictive analytics: forecasting sales, demand, or trends based on historical data
    - recommendation systems: personalizing recommendations in e-commerce or content-streaming platforms.
    - natural language processing: understanding and processing human language in chatbots, translation, sentiment analysis, etc.

Deep Learning

Definition: Deep learning is a subset of ML that uses neural networks with multiple layers to model and process complex patterns in data. It aims to mimic the human brain's structure and function in learning and decision-making.

- Key Components
  - neural networks: composed of interconnected nodes (neurons) organized in layers (input, hidden, output)
  - Layers: deep architectures consisting of multiple hidden layers allowing for hierarchical abstraction of data

- Applications
  - computer vision: object detection, image recognition, and video analysis
  - natural language processing: language translation, sentiment analysis, and chatbots
  - autonomous vehicles: processing sensor data for decision-making in self-driving cars

Neural Networks

Definition: Neural networks are computing systems inspired by the biological neural networks of the human brain. They consist of interconnected nodes, or artificial neurons, that process information by transmitting signals.

- Types of Neural Networks
  - Feedforward neural networks: Information flows in one direction, from input nodes through hidden nodes to output nodes.
  - Recurrent neural networks (RNN): Designed to work with sequence data, having connections looping back, enabling them to retain information.

- Convolutional neural networks (CNN): Specialized for processing gridlike data, such as images or videos, by applying convolution operations.

- Applications
  - Image recognition: Identifying objects, faces, or patterns in images.
  - Speech recognition: Transcribing spoken language into text.
  - Time series prediction: Forecasting based on sequential data.

Understanding these concepts provides a foundational understanding of how AI systems learn, process information, and make decisions, underpinning the myriad applications revolutionizing industries today.

AI's Role in Automation and Decision-Making

AI plays a pivotal role in both automation and decision-making across various industries, revolutionizing processes, improving efficiency, and augmenting human capabilities.

Automation

- Streamlining repetitive tasks: AI automates routine and repetitive tasks, allowing businesses to optimize processes by reducing manual labor and errors.
- Increased efficiency: Automation through AI leads to enhanced operational efficiency as AI-powered systems can perform tasks faster and more accurately than humans.
- Scalability: AI-driven automation allows for scalable solutions, enabling businesses to handle increased workloads without a proportional increase in resources.
- Examples: Robotic process automation (RPA) in finance for automating data entry, chatbots handling customer service inquiries, and AI-driven machinery in manufacturing for production tasks.

Decision-Making

- Data-driven insights: AI processes vast amounts of data to generate insights, empowering businesses to make informed decisions based on data-driven intelligence.
- Predictive analytics: AI models forecast trends, patterns, and future outcomes, aiding in strategic decision-making by providing predictive insights.
- Personalized recommendations: AI-driven recommendation systems analyze user behavior to offer personalized recommendations, enhancing customer experience and driving sales.
- Real-time decision support: AI systems process information rapidly, enabling real-time decision support in critical scenarios like fraud detection in finance and patient diagnosis in health care.

AI-Augmented Decision-Making

- Enhanced accuracy: AI assists decision-making by analyzing large datasets and identifying patterns that humans might overlook, leading to more accurate decisions.
- Risk mitigation: AI models assess risks by analyzing historical data, enabling businesses to identify potential risks and take preventive measures.
- Continuous learning: AI systems learn and adapt continuously from new data, refining their decision-making abilities over time.
- Human-AI collaboration: AI augments human decision-making rather than replacing it, allowing for a collaborative approach whereby AI systems support human expertise.

Conclusion

AI's integration into automation and decision-making processes reshapes industries by enhancing efficiency, enabling scalability, and providing valuable insights. As AI technology advances, its role in automation and decision-making continues to evolve, offering businesses unprecedented opportunities to innovate, optimize operations, and gain a competitive edge in an increasingly data-driven and dynamic business landscape.

Chapter 3

Data and AI

Understanding the Foundation: Data as the Lifeblood of AI

Data as Fuel for AI

- Fundamental building block: Explain how data serves as the foundation for AI systems, enabling them to learn, improve, and make accurate predictions.
- Quality versus quantity: Discuss the significance of both data quality and quantity in training AI models. Emphasize the need for clean, diverse, and ample datasets.

Types of Data in AI Integration

- Structured versus unstructured data: Differentiate between structured data (easily organized into databases) and unstructured data (text, images, videos), highlighting their respective roles in AI applications.
- Streaming data: Explain the importance of real-time streaming data for AI systems in making immediate decisions.

Data Preprocessing and Cleaning

- Data preparation pipeline: Illustrate the process of data preprocessing, including cleaning, normalization, and feature engineering, to ensure the data's suitability for AI model training.
- Challenges and solutions: Discuss common challenges in data preprocessing and strategies to overcome them to maintain data integrity.

Data Privacy and Ethics

- Ethical considerations: Highlight the ethical implications of using data in AI, emphasizing the importance of privacy, fairness, and transparency in data usage.
- Regulatory compliance: Discuss regulatory frameworks (like GDPR) and guidelines ensuring responsible data handling in AI applications.

Data Governance and Management

- Importance of governance: Emphasize the significance of robust data governance policies and practices to ensure data quality, security, and compliance.
- Data life cycle management: Explore the life cycle of data from collection to disposal, focusing on best practices for its efficient management.

Data Partnerships and Acquisition

- Collaborative data initiatives: Discuss the trend of collaborative data initiatives and partnerships among businesses to access diverse datasets and foster innovation.
- Data acquisition strategies: Highlight the strategies for acquiring relevant data, including in-house collection, partnerships, or third-party sources.

Conclusion

Data Collection, Storage, and Management for AI Initiatives

Emphasize that data stands as the cornerstone of AI integration, underscoring its critical role in training, refining, and empowering AI systems. The chapter aims to illuminate the significance of clean, diverse, and ethically handled data, serving as the backbone for successful AI implementation across various industries.

Data Collection Strategies

a. Types of Data Sources

- Internal data: Discuss leveraging in-house data from various departments and systems within an organization.
- External data: Explore acquiring data from external sources like open data repositories, API, or third-party vendors.

b. Data Collection Methods

- Passive versus active collection: Differentiate between passive collection (automated collection from existing sources) and active collection (intentional gathering through surveys, feedback, etc.).
- IoT and sensor data: Highlight the role of IoT devices and sensors in generating real-time, continuous data streams.

2. Data Storage and Infrastructure

a. Storage Systems

- Traditional versus cloud storage: Compare traditional on-premises storage with cloud-based solutions, discussing the advantages and considerations of each.
- Big data technologies: Introduce technologies like Hadoop, Spark, and NoSQL databases for handling large volumes of diverse data.

b. Scalability and Security

- Scalable architectures: Discuss scalable storage architectures to accommodate increasing data volumes and ensure performance.
- Data security measures: Highlight encryption, access controls, and data masking to protect sensitive information.

Data Management Best Practices

a. Data Quality and Governance

   • Data quality assurance: Discuss strategies for maintaining high-quality data through validation, cleaning, and consistency checks.
   • Governance frameworks: Emphasize the importance of governance frameworks for managing data access, privacy, and compliance.

b. Metadata and Cataloging

   • Metadata importance: Explain the role of metadata in data management, aiding in data discovery, lineage, and understanding.
   • Data catalogs: Introduce data catalogs as a means to organize, categorize, and index available data assets.

Chapter 4

Ethics and Responsibility in AI

Understanding Ethical Considerations in AI Applications

Understanding ethical considerations in AI involves recognizing and addressing various moral implications associated with developing, deploying, and using artificial intelligence. Here are some key points:

- Fairness and bias: Ensuring AI systems make fair decisions and don't perpetuate biases based on race, gender, or other factors. Addressing biases in datasets and algorithms is crucial.
- Transparency and explainability: Making AI systems transparent and understandable, allowing users to comprehend how decisions are made. This helps build trust and accountability.
- Privacy and consent: Respecting user privacy by implementing robust data protection measures and obtaining informed consent for data collection and usage.
- Accountability and responsibility: Assigning accountability when AI systems cause harm and establishing guidelines for responsible development and deployment of AI technologies.
- Social and economic implications: Considering the broader societal impact of AI, including its effects on employment, social equity, and access to resources.
- Human-centric approach: Prioritizing human values, dignity, and wellbeing in the design and application of AI systems, ensuring they serve human interests ethically.
- Regulations and standards: Advocating for regulatory frameworks and industry standards to govern AI development and usage, ensuring compliance with ethical guidelines.

Understanding these ethical considerations is essential to navigate the ethical challenges posed by AI and to create frameworks that promote responsible and ethical AI development and implementation.

Responsible AI Development and Implementation

Research on responsible AI development and implementation spans various disciplines like computer science, ethics, law, and sociology. Some notable areas of research include the following:

- ethical frameworks: Developing and refining ethical guidelines and frameworks that address the moral implications of AI systems in society.
- fairness and bias mitigation: Studying methods to detect, mitigate, and prevent biases in AI algorithms to ensure fair and unbiased decision-making.
- explainable AI (XAI): Investigating techniques to make AI models more interpretable and transparent, enabling users to understand how AI reaches conclusions.
- privacy-preserving AI: Exploring methods to protect user data and privacy while maintaining the effectiveness of AI systems.
- accountability and governance: Researching legal and regulatory frameworks to hold developers and users accountable for AI systems' actions.
- human-AI interaction: Studying how humans interact with AI systems, including user trust, collaboration, and user-friendly interfaces.
- socioeconomic impact: Analyzing the broader societal impact of AI deployment, including workforce changes, economic disparities, and ethical implications.
- cross-disciplinary collaboration: Encouraging collaboration among different fields to address the complex challenges of responsible AI development.

Researchers aim to create a comprehensive understanding of the ethical, societal, and technical aspects of AI development to ensure its responsible and beneficial integration into various domains. Numerous academic institutions, think tanks, and industry leaders are actively contributing to this evolving field through their research efforts.

Implementing AI Strategies

Chapter 5

AI Adoption Road Map

Understand Business Objectives

- Define clear business objectives that AI can help achieve.
- Align AI initiatives with the overall strategic goals of the organization.

Leadership Alignment

- Ensure leadership commitment and support for AI integration.
- Communicate the benefits of AI adoption to key stakeholders.

Data Assessment

- Evaluate the quality, quantity, and relevance of existing data.
- Identify data sources and assess data governance and security measures.

Infrastructure Evaluation

- Assess the current IT infrastructure's capability to support AI implementation.
- Consider cloud services, on-premises solutions, or hybrid models.

Skills and Talent Gap Analysis

- Identify the skills needed for AI integration.
- Assess the current skill set within the organization and plan for training or hiring as necessary.

Regulatory Compliance

- Understand and comply with data protection and privacy regulations.
- Ensure that AI implementation adheres to legal and ethical standards.

Risk Management

- Identify potential risks associated with AI implementation.
- Develop strategies to mitigate risks and establish contingency plans.

Proof of Concept (PoC)

- Conduct a small-scale PoC to demonstrate the feasibility and benefits of AI.
- Use the PoC to gather feedback and make necessary adjustments.

Vendor Selection

- Evaluate AI solution providers and technologies.
- Consider factors such as scalability, flexibility, and ongoing support.

Integration Planning

- Develop a phased integration plan.
- Prioritize AI initiatives based on business impact and complexity.

Change Management

- Implement a change-management strategy to facilitate a smooth transition.
- Communicate changes effectively and provide training and support.

Monitoring and Evaluation

- Establish key performance indicators (KPI) to measure the success of AI integration.
- Implement monitoring tools and regularly evaluate the performance of AI systems.

Scalability

- Ensure that the AI solutions can scale as the organization grows.
- Plan for future enhancements and advancements in AI technology.

Continuous Improvement

- Foster a culture of continuous improvement.
- Iterate on AI models and processes based on feedback and evolving business needs.

Documentation

- Document the entire AI adoption process, including decisions, challenges, and solutions.
- Create a knowledge repository for ongoing reference.

Community and Industry Engagement

- Stay connected with the AI community and industry trends.
- Participate in conferences and forums and collaborate with peers to stay informed.

By following these steps, you can create a robust AI adoption road map that aligns with your organization's goals and ensures a successful integration of AI technologies. Keep in mind that AI adoption is an ongoing process, and regular assessments and adjustments will be necessary to adapt to changing circumstances and advancements in AI technology.

Chapter 6

AI Implementation and Integration

Developing AI strategies aligned with business goals involves a systematic approach that integrates AI technologies with the overall objectives of the organization. Here's a step-by-step guide to help you formulate AI strategies that align with business goals:

Define Business Objectives

- Clearly articulate the business goals and objectives that AI is expected to support.
- Align AI initiatives with the overarching mission and vision of the organization.

Understand Industry Landscape

- Conduct a thorough analysis of the industry landscape to identify trends, challenges, and opportunities.
- Evaluate how AI can provide a competitive advantage within the industry.

Identify Key Performance Indicators (KPI)

- Determine the key metrics that reflect the success of your business goals.
- Establish measurable KPI that AI initiatives will impact.

Evaluate Current Capabilities

- Assess the current state of technology, data infrastructure, and workforce skills.
- Identify areas where AI can enhance or complement existing capabilities.

Prioritize Use Cases

- Identify specific AI use cases that align with business objectives and have a high impact.
- Prioritize use cases based on feasibility, business value, and resource requirements.

Data Strategy

- Develop a comprehensive data strategy that aligns with business goals.
- Ensure data quality, security, and accessibility for AI applications.

Technology Stack Selection

- Evaluate and choose appropriate AI technologies based on the identified use cases.
- Consider factors such as scalability, compatibility, and integration with existing systems.

Investment Planning

- Develop a budget for AI initiatives, considering costs for technology, talent, and infrastructure.
- Prioritize investments based on their alignment with high-impact business goals.

Talent Acquisition and Development

- Identify the skills and expertise required for successful AI implementation.
- Invest in training existing employees and hiring skilled professionals as needed.

By following these steps, organizations can develop AI strategies that are not only aligned with business goals but also adaptable to evolving market conditions and technological advancements. Regular evaluation and adjustment of the AI strategy will help ensure its continued relevance and effectiveness.

Selecting the right AI tools for business needs involves a systematic process that considers various factors to ensure alignment with organizational objectives. Here's a step-by-step guide:

Understand Business Objectives

- Define objectives: Clearly articulate the specific business goals and objectives that AI tools are expected to support.
- Alignment: Ensure that the selected AI tools align with the overall strategic vision and mission of the organization.

Conduct a Needs Assessment

- Identify pain points: Understand the existing challenges and pain points within the organization that AI can address.
- Stakeholder involvement: Involve key stakeholders, including business leaders and end users, in the assessment process.

Evaluate Data Readiness

- Assess data availability: Evaluate the quality, quantity, and relevance of available data.
- Data governance: Ensure proper data governance, security, and compliance with regulations.

Define Key Performance Indicators (KPI)

- Quantifiable metrics: Establish measurable KPI that reflect the success of AI implementations.
- Benchmarking: Use benchmarks to set realistic expectations for AI performance.

Identify AI Use Cases

- Prioritize use cases: Identify specific use cases where AI can provide the most significant business impact.
- Feasibility analysis: Assess the technical and organizational feasibility of implementing AI for each use case.

Consider Scalability and Integration

- Scalability: Evaluate whether the selected AI tools can scale with the organization's growth.
- Integration: Ensure seamless integration with existing systems and workflows.

Evaluate Vendor Solutions

- Market research: Research and compare AI tool vendors based on their reputation, customer reviews, and market presence.
- Trial periods: Consider trial periods or proof-of-concept projects to assess the tools' effectiveness in a real business environment.

Assess Customization and Flexibility

- Customization options: Evaluate the level of customization the AI tools offer to meet specific business requirements.
- Adaptability: Ensure that the tools can adapt to changing business needs and evolving technology.

Consider User Experience

- User-friendliness: Assess the user interface and overall user experience of the AI tools.
- Training requirements: Consider the ease of training for employees who will be using the tools.

Evaluate Costs and ROI

- Total cost of ownership (TCO): Consider the overall cost of implementing and maintaining the AI tools.
- ROI analysis: Assess the potential return on investment based on expected business outcomes.

Account for Ethical Considerations

- Bias and fairness: Evaluate the AI tools for potential biases and fairness issues.
- Ethical use: Ensure that the tools adhere to ethical standards and comply with regulatory requirements.

Assess Technical Support and Maintenance

- Support availability: Ensure that the vendor provides adequate technical support.
- Maintenance: Assess the frequency and nature of updates and maintenance requirements.

Pilot Implementation

- Small-scale deployment: Consider implementing the selected AI tools on a small scale or in a controlled environment.
- Gather feedback: Collect feedback from users and stakeholders during the pilot phase.

Iterative Improvement

- Continuous feedback: Establish a feedback loop for continuous improvement based on user feedback and evolving business needs.
- Iterate as needed: Be prepared to iterate on the AI tools and processes for optimization.

Document the Selection Process

- Create a selection document: Document the entire AI tool selection process, including criteria, evaluations, and decisions made.
- Knowledge transfer: Ensure knowledge transfer to relevant teams for ongoing support and management.

Stay Informed about AI Trends

- Continuous learning: Stay abreast of the latest trends and advancements in AI technology.
- Futureproofing: Select tools with a road map for future enhancements and capabilities.

By following these steps, organizations can establish a robust and well-informed process for selecting AI tools that effectively meet their specific business needs. Regular assessments and adjustments to the tool set should be made to keep pace with technological advancements and changing business requirements.

Implementing AI in a business environment can pose various challenges, ranging from technical complexities to organizational resistance. Overcoming these challenges requires a strategic and holistic approach. Here's a guide on how to address common challenges in implementing AI:

Cultural and Organizational Challenges

- Leadership Buy-In
  - Solution: Secure support from top leadership. Communicate the strategic importance of AI and its potential impact on business goals.

- Employee Resistance
  - Solution: Implement change management strategies. Involve employees in the process, provide training, and communicate the benefits of AI adoption.

Data-Related Challenges

- Data Quality and Availability
  - Solution: Conduct a thorough data assessment. Invest in data cleaning, enrichment, and ensure the availability of high-quality data.

- Data Security and Privacy Concerns
  - Solution: Implement robust data governance policies. Adhere to privacy regulations and use encryption and secure data storage solutions.

Technical Challenges

- Integration with Existing Systems
  - Solution: Plan for seamless integration by using API and middleware. Choose AI tools that are compatible with existing infrastructure.

- Scalability
  - Solution: Select scalable AI solutions that can grow with the organization. Plan for future expansion and increasing data volumes.

Talent and Skills Gap

- Lack of In-House Expertise
  - Solution: Invest in training programs for existing employees. Consider hiring AI specialists or partnering with external experts and vendors.

- Rapid Technological Advancements
  - Solution: Foster a culture of continuous learning. Encourage employees to stay updated on AI trends through training, workshops, and conferences.

Cost and ROI Concerns

- High Implementation Costs
  - Solution: Develop a comprehensive budget that includes implementation, training, and ongoing maintenance costs. Consider the long-term return on investment.

- Demonstrating ROI
  - Solution: Establish clear KPI and regularly evaluate AI's impact on business outcomes. Communicate success stories and quantify the benefits.

Ethical and Bias-Related Challenges

- Biased Models
  - Solution: Regularly audit and monitor AI models for biases. Use diverse datasets and implement fairness-aware algorithms.

- Ethical Use of AI
  - Solution: Develop ethical guidelines for AI use within the organization. Ensure compliance with legal and regulatory frameworks.

Regulatory Compliance

- Navigating Legal Frameworks
  - Solution: Stay informed about data protection and privacy regulations. Work with legal experts to ensure compliance and adjust strategies accordingly.

- International Regulations
  - Solution: Understand and adhere to international regulations if operating in multiple jurisdictions. Develop a global compliance strategy.

Communication Challenges

- Explaining AI to Nontechnical Stakeholders
  - Solution: Develop clear and concise communication strategies. Use demonstrations, case studies, and visuals to illustrate the benefits of AI.

- Aligning AI with Business Objectives
  - Solution: Regularly communicate how AI initiatives align with overall business goals. Use performance metrics to demonstrate progress.

Security Concerns

- Vulnerability to Cyberthreats
  - Solution: Implement robust cybersecurity measures. Regularly update security protocols and collaborate with IT security experts.

- Protecting Sensitive Data
  - Solution: Use encryption, access controls, and anonymization techniques to protect sensitive data. Ensure compliance with industry-specific security standards.

Collaboration Challenges

- Silos in Departments
  - Solution: Foster cross-functional collaboration. Encourage open communication and shared goals across departments.

- External Collaboration
  - Solution: Collaborate with external partners, vendors, and industry experts. Leverage external knowledge and resources.

Overcoming Bias in Decision-Making

- Human Intervention
  - Solution: Incorporate human oversight in AI decision-making. Establish clear guidelines for handling biased outputs.

- Transparency
  - Solution: Make AI decision-making processes transparent. Clearly communicate how decisions are reached to build trust.

Adapting to Change

- Resilience to Change
  - Solution: Promote a culture of adaptability. Highlight the benefits of change and how it contributes to long-term success.

- Continuous Improvement
  - Solution: Encourage a mindset of continuous improvement. Regularly assess and update AI strategies to align with evolving business needs.

Chapter 7

AI-Driven Business Models

Rethinking Business Models with AI

Addressing these challenges requires a multidimensional approach that considers technological, organizational, and ethical aspects. A proactive and flexible strategy, coupled with ongoing evaluation and refinement, is key to successful AI implementation in a business context.

Implementing AI in a business environment can pose various challenges, ranging from technical complexities to organizational resistance. Overcoming these challenges requires a strategic and holistic approach. Here's a guide on how to address common challenges in implementing AI:

Cultural and Organizational Challenges

- Leadership Buy-In
  - Solution: Secure support from top leadership. Communicate the strategic importance of AI and its potential impact on business goals.

- Employee Resistance
  - Solution: Implement change management strategies. Involve employees in the process, provide training, and communicate the benefits of AI adoption.

Data-related Challenges

- Data Quality and Availability
  - Solution: Conduct a thorough data assessment Invest in data cleaning, enrichment and ensure the availability of high-quality data.

- Data Security and Privacy Concerns
  - Solution: Implement robust data governance policies. Adhere to privacy regulations and use encryption and secure data storage solutions.

Technical Challenges

- Integration with Existing Systems
  - Solution: Plan for seamless integration by using API and middleware. Choose AI tools that are compatible with existing infrastructure.

- Scalability
  - Solution: Select scalable AI solutions that can grow with the organization. Plan for future expansion and increasing data volumes.

Talent and Skills Gap

- Lack of In-House Expertise
  - Solution: Invest in training programs for existing employees. Consider hiring AI specialists or partnering with external experts and vendors.

- Rapid Technological Advancements
  - Solution: Foster a culture of continuous learning. Encourage employees to stay updated on AI trends through training, workshops, and conferences.

Cost and ROI Concerns

- High Implementation Costs
  - Solution: Develop a comprehensive budget that includes implementation, training, and ongoing maintenance costs. Consider the long-term return on investment.

- Demonstrating ROI
  - Solution: Establish clear KPI and regularly evaluate AI's impact on business outcomes. Communicate success stories and quantify the benefits.

Ethical and Bias-related Challenges

- Biased Models
  - Solution: Regularly audit and monitor AI models for biases. Use diverse datasets and implement fairness-aware algorithms.

- Ethical Use of AI
  - Solution: Develop ethical guidelines for AI use within the organization. Ensure compliance with legal and regulatory frameworks.

Regulatory Compliance

- Navigating Legal Frameworks
  - Solution: Stay informed about data protection and privacy regulations. Work with legal experts to ensure compliance and adjust strategies accordingly.

- International Regulations
  - Solution: Understand and adhere to international regulations if operating in multiple jurisdictions. Develop a global compliance strategy.

Communication Challenges

- Explaining AI to Nontechnical Stakeholders
  - Solution: Develop clear and concise communication strategies. Use demonstrations, case studies, and visuals to illustrate the benefits of AI.

- Aligning AI with Business Objectives
  - Solution: Regularly communicate how AI initiatives align with overall business goals. Use performance metrics to demonstrate progress.

Security Concerns

- Vulnerability to Cyberthreats
  - Solution: Implement robust cybersecurity measures. Regularly update security protocols and collaborate with IT security experts.

- Protecting Sensitive Data
  - Solution: Use encryption, access controls, and anonymization techniques to protect sensitive data. Ensure compliance with industry-specific security standards.

Collaboration Challenges

- Silos in Departments
  - Solution: Foster cross-functional collaboration. Encourage open communication and shared goals across departments.

- External Collaboration
  - Solution: Collaborate with external partners, vendors, and industry experts. Leverage external knowledge and resources.

Overcoming Bias in Decision-Making

- Human Intervention
  - Solution: Incorporate human oversight in AI decision-making. Establish clear guidelines for handling biased outputs.

- Transparency
  - Solution: Make AI decision-making processes transparent. Clearly communicate how decisions are reached to build trust.

Adapting to Change

- Resilience to Change
  - Solution: Promote a culture of adaptability. Highlight the benefits of change and how it contributes to long-term success.

- Continuous Improvement
  - Solution: Encourage a mindset of continuous improvement. Regularly assess and update AI strategies to align with evolving business needs.

Addressing these challenges requires a multidimensional approach that considers technological, organizational, and ethical aspects. A proactive and flexible strategy, coupled with ongoing evaluation and refinement, is key to successful AI implementation in a business context.

Rethinking business models in AI involves considering how artificial intelligence can fundamentally transform the way businesses create, deliver, and capture value. Here's a guide on exploring new business models in the context of AI research:

- AI's transformative potential: Highlight how AI technologies have the potential to revolutionize traditional business models across various industries.
- Need for rethinking: Discuss the necessity of rethinking business models to harness the full potential of AI.

Understanding AI Capabilities

- Data analysis and insights: Explore how AI can generate valuable insights from large datasets, enabling better decision-making.
- Automation and efficiency: Discuss AI's role in automating processes, improving operational efficiency, and reducing costs.

Identifying Industry-Specific Opportunities

- Customization for industries: Recognize that AI applications can vary across industries. Identify industry-specific opportunities for AI integration.
- Market trends: Analyze current market trends and demands that AI can address within specific sectors.

Exploring Monetization Strategies

- Subscription models: Consider offering AI solutions through subscription-based models, providing ongoing access to AI-driven insights or services.
- Pay-per-use: Implement pay-per-use or pay-per-result models, especially for AI applications with variable usage patterns.

Collaboration and Ecosystem Building

- Partnerships and alliances: Explore collaborations with other businesses, startups, or tech giants to build a comprehensive AI ecosystem.
- API and integrations: Provide API for seamless integration of AI capabilities into existing business processes and platforms.

Value-based Pricing

- Demonstrating value: Clearly communicate the value proposition of AI solutions to customers.
- Value-based pricing: Consider pricing models based on the perceived value delivered to customers rather than traditional cost-based models.

Data Monetization

- Leveraging data assets: Explore ways to monetize data assets generated through AI applications.
- Anonymized data sales: Consider selling anonymized and aggregated data to third parties, adhering to privacy regulations.

AI-Driven Personalization

- Tailored customer experiences: Use AI to deliver highly personalized products or services.
- Subscription boxes and services: Implement subscription box or service models based on AI-driven personalization.

Outcome-Based Models

- Guaranteed outcomes: Offer guarantees or commitments tied to specific outcomes facilitated by AI applications.
- Risk-sharing models: Explore models where risks and rewards are shared with customers based on AI-driven predictions or recommendations.

Building AI Platforms

- Platform as a service (PaaS): Develop AI platforms that allow businesses to build, deploy, and manage their AI applications.
- Marketplace models: Create marketplaces where AI solutions, algorithms, or datasets can be bought and sold.

Sustainability-focused Models

- Energy-efficient AI: Develop and promote AI models that prioritize energy efficiency, catering to environmentally conscious customers.
- Sustainable supply chains: Implement AI-driven models for optimizing supply chains with a focus on sustainability.

Ethical Considerations

- Responsible AI practices: Emphasize ethical AI practices and transparency in your business model.
- Customer trust: Build trust by clearly communicating how AI is used, addressing biases, and ensuring user privacy.

Continuous Innovation

- Agile development: Embrace agile development methodologies to continuously iterate and improve AI-driven products and services.
- Open innovation: Foster an environment of open innovation, encouraging ideas from both within and outside the organization.

Regulatory Compliance

- Understanding regulations: Stay informed about evolving AI regulations and ensure compliance in the business model.
- Ethical guidelines: Develop internal ethical guidelines for AI use and incorporate them into the business model.

Case Studies and Best Practices

- Real-world examples: Provide case studies showcasing businesses successfully implementing new AI-driven business models.
- Learn from failures: Analyze failures and challenges faced by others in the industry to avoid common pitfalls.

Conclusion

- Summary of rethinking business models: Summarize the key points on rethinking business models with AI.
- Call to action: Encourage businesses to explore and experiment with innovative AI-driven business models.

Chapter 8

Research and Leadership in the AI World

Research and Leadership in the AI World

Leadership in an AI-powered world involves navigating complexities while harnessing the potential of AI for organizational success. Effective leaders need to do the following:

- Align AI initiatives with organizational goals, ensuring a clear strategy for implementation and growth using strategic integration.
- Establish ethical guidelines for AI use, promoting responsible development and deployment to mitigate risks and biases.
- Cultivate a workforce with AI literacy and adaptability, fostering a culture that embraces learning and innovation through skill development.
- Encourage collaboration between humans and AI systems, leveraging their complementary strengths for enhanced productivity and creativity and collaboration culture.
- Embrace change by staying abreast of AI advancements, fostering agility and adaptability to evolve alongside technological developments and continuous adaptation.

Leadership in an AI-powered era requires a blend of technical understanding, strategic vision, ethical considerations, and a people-centric approach to maximize the potential of AI while addressing its challenges.

- Leadership adaptation: Analyzing how leaders adapt their strategies and styles in response to AI integration within organizations.

- Decision-making and AI: Investigating how AI influences leadership decision-making processes, including the augmentation of human decision-making with AI insights.
- Assessing the impact of AI on organizational structures, cultures, and hierarchies and how leaders navigate these changes.
- Identifying the key skills and competencies leaders need to effectively leverage AI in leaders need to effectively leverage AI within their leadership approaches.
- Examining the ethical considerations of using AI in leadership, including issues related to bias, transparency, and accountability.

Incorporating real-world case studies and best practices of leaders effectively utilizes AI in their leadership strategies across different industries. Leadership in AI decision-making assists in navigating ethical, strategic, and societal implications. This provides an overview of AI's growing influence in decision-making processes, including the importance of ethical leadership in AI-driven decision-making, understanding AI decision-making, an explanation of AI algorithms and their role in decision-making.

Also included are types of AI decision-making systems (supervised learning, reinforcement learning), challenges and biases in AI decision-making (algorithmic bias, fairness, transparency), leadership in AI decision-making, the role of human leaders in guiding AI based decisions, ethical considerations and the responsibility of leadership in AI deployment. Strategies for ethical leadership in AI decision-making (diversity in AI teams, ethical frameworks, governance) are discussed.

Leadership in AI Decision-Making

- role of human leaders in guiding AI-based decisions
- ethical considerations and the responsibilities of leadership in AI deployment
- strategies for ethical leadership in AI decision-making (diversity in AI teams, ethical frameworks, governance
- impact on society and organizations

- societal implications of AI decision-making (employment, privacy, bias)
- business implications and competitiveness advantage through ethical AI leadership
- case studies/examples of successful and ethical AI leadership in decision-making
- challenges and future directions
- current challenges in implementing ethical AI decision-making processes
- future trends in AI leadership and decision-making (explainable AI, AI regulation, etc.)
- recommendation for fostering better AI leadership in decision-making contexts

Conclusion

- recap of the importance of ethical leadership in AI decision-making
- final thoughts on the role of leaders in shaping the future of AI decision-making
- Ensure you gather credible sources and research studies to support your points. Consider exploring real-world examples of companies or organizations that have effectively navigated ethical challenges in AI decision-making.

Chapter 9

Leadership in the AI World

Leadership in the AI World

Leadership in an AI-powered world involves navigating complexities while harnessing the potential of AI for organizational success. Effective leaders need to

- align AI initiatives with organizational goals, ensuring a clear strategy for implementation and growth using strategic integration
- establish ethical guidelines for AI use, promoting responsible development and deployment to mitigate risks and biases
- cultivate a workforce with AI literacy and adaptability, fostering a culture that embraces learning and innovation through skill development
- encourage collaboration between humans and AI systems, leveraging their complementary strengths for enhanced productivity and creativity and collaboration culture
- embrace change by staying abreast of AI advancements, fostering agility and adaptability to evolve alongside technological developments and continuous adaptation

Leadership in an AI-powered era requires a blend of technical understanding, strategic vision, ethical considerations, and a people-centric approach to maximize the potential of AI while addressing its challenges.

- leadership adaptation: analyzing how leaders adapt their strategies and styles in response to AI integration within organizations
- decision-making and AI: investigating how AI influences leadership decision-making processes, including the augmentation of human decision-making with AI insights

- assessing the impact of AI on organizational structures, cultures, and hierarchies and how leaders navigate these changes
- identifying the key skills and competencies leaders need to effectively leverage AI in leaders need to effectively leverage AI within their leadership approaches
- examining the ethical considerations of using AI in leadership, including issues related to bias, transparency, and accountability

Incorporating real-world case studies and best practices of leaders effectively utilizing AI in their leadership strategies across different industries needs to be catalogued and researched. Leadership in AI decision-making navigating ethical, strategic, and societal implications should be a priority of research. AI's growing influence in decision-making processes along with the importance of ethical leadership in AI-driven decision-making provides reports for leaders and insight into how future leaders navigate changes in organizational structures.

Understanding AI decision-making can help to assist in effectively leveraging AI leadership approaches and key skills and competencies. Explanation of AI algorithms and their role in decision-making assist in leveraging complementary strengths for enhanced productivity and collaborative culture. Challenges and biases in AI decision-making, such as algorithmic bias, fairness, and transparency, need further research to ensure ethical social impact and responsible use of the AI tools in organizations. Types of AI decision-making systems, supervised learning, reinforcement learning, and training systems for existing employees. Leadership in AI decision-making of human leaders in guiding AI-based decisions help foster cross-functional collaboration, encourage open communication, and share goals across departments. Ethical considerations and the responsibility of leadership in AI deployment promote a culture of adaptability while benefiting continuous improvement and contributing to long-term successes. Strategies for ethical leadership in AI decision-making encourage diversity in AI teams and ethical frameworks and provide additional tools for governance.

AI Research and Digital Leadership

Data is usually collected using a wide range of methods that include questionnaires, interviews, reviews of school plans, community focus groups, and participatory discussion groups. There are multiple methods to retrieve data and predict trends. The diffusion of innovation theory is a valuable model that has been used to guide technological innovation and advancement.

The evidence-based medical model has been adapted in ways to meet the technological advances of today.

Focusing on leadership, theory, management practices, and peer networking along with meeting the needs of networking and adoption of new tools like machine learning and AI. Machine learning is generated using algorithms to review data and predict trends. In AI there is a continuous feed of data, and machine learning (ML) is a specific branch of artificial intelligence (AI).

ML has a limited scope and focus compared to AI. AI includes several strategies and technologies that are outside the scope of machine learning. The digital transformation age refers to the adoption of technologies throughout multiple sectors but focuses on data science, which is managing, processing, and interpreting information in digital platforms, decision-making, artificial intelligence, machine learning, and big data. The use of machine learning is generated using algorithms to review data and predict trends.

In AI there is a continuous feed of data, and machine learning (ML) is a specific branch of artificial intelligence (AI). ML has a limited scope and focus compared to AI. AI includes several strategies and technologies that are outside the scope of machine learning. Digital leadership theory along with the use of evidence-based medical models can be applied in businesses, organizations, and universities to achieve business goals and develop strategic plans.

The adoption of electronic health records as well as electronic note-taking in health care brought about an early adoption of digital data analysis collection through digital platforms. The digital theory with the use of the evidence-based practice evidence-based medical model is a template for framing how artificial intelligence can assist with data analysis in management, education, and marketing sectors of training, leadership, research, policy, and development.

The digital transformation age refers to the adoption of technologies throughout multiple sectors but focuses on data science, which is managing, processing, and interpreting information in digital platforms, decision-making, artificial intelligence, machine learning, and big data. Machine learning is generated using algorithms to review data and predict trends.

In AI there is a continuous feed of data, and machine learning (ML) is a specific branch of artificial intelligence (AI).

ML has a limited scope and focus compared to AI. AI includes several strategies and technologies that are outside the scope of machine learning.

Digital leadership theory can be applied in businesses, organizations, and universities to achieve business goals and develop strategic plans.

A greater understanding of how evidence-based practice theory along with inclusive education can be used in workforce training, policy development, research leadership, and data analysis to collect meaningful data using both the internet and artificial intelligence machine learning mechanisms. Focus on sustainability in performance, inclusion, and evidence practice with digital AI in management, marketing, and educational services. Research is important in framing how artificial intelligence can assist with data analysis in management, education, and marketing sectors of training, leadership, research, policy, and development.

Educational Research and Transformational Leadership

AI in online executive education courses and AI's applicability in supporting leaders' learning are needed to augment the body of knowledge in the field of organizational leadership by examining organizational leaders' and instructors' perceptions of AI to online executive education courses the workplace. Studying transformational leadership in the workplace does the following:

- helps organizations realize new sources of value beyond the limited application in the workplace
- enhances the efficiency and efficacy of online executive education courses and the organizational adoption of AI concepts and tools from online executive education courses

There are many beneficial uses of AI in the workplace that could affect organizational learning and executive online tools for learning. Providing research on how AI can attempt to solve business problems and impact organizational learning is a new body of research that has not fully been studied. Enhancing the efficiency and efficacy of online executive education courses while focusing on practice instead of theory in student and executive learning outcomes and delivery of course content will enhance the body of knowledge and evidence-based outcomes.

Online collaborative learning and systems, and AI as a technology to instructors and students, allowed the research to address questions and perceptions. AI applications such as online executive education courses improve instruction and support organizational leader learning. Additional studies are needed to improve awareness of the field of online education and AI use by exploring leaders' and instructors' perceptions about the utility of AI in online executive courses. Future research should include quantitative and qualitative effects on the experiences of instructors and organizational leaders. AI research can attempt to solve business problems, impact organizational learning, and focus on culturally appropriate topics in an interactive course is a new body of research that has not yet been studied.

AI is transforming the world, and technology is necessary to remain competitive. The Department of Defense (DOD) is investing billions of dollars to incorporate AI technologies into military operations as warfare is changing and AI is needed to win future conflicts. The theory of diffusion of innovation model is one method used to communicate how technology and information can be adopted and communicated over time. Additional research needs to be completed on

- technology acceptance models
- attitude-behavior relationship
- and transformational leadership

Future studies should expand to explore other services and civilian counterparts.

Current research concludes that followers' attitudes toward AI were influenced by their immediate supervisors' transformational leadership abilities. The study also found that the relationship between one's perceived knowledge of a technology and one's attitude toward it remains the same when used or changed to AI (Reeves, 2023). Reeves found that the followers' rating of their immediate supervisors' attitudes toward AI was a statistically significant predictor of their attitudes toward AI. Reeves did find that idealized attitudes negatively affected the participants' attitudes toward AI for 160 participants.

In fulfilling society's needs using an inclusion conceptional framework and functional theory, Felder (2018) indicated the necessity for transformational educational research and system change. In using functional theory, the inclusive education model demonstrated positive outcomes on student achievement and socialization. This design emphasized inclusivity in the classroom for children with disabilities but also focused on inclusive classrooms that focused on positive motivation for children with different attributes. These attributes included ethnicity, language, gender, and socioeconomic status.

The inclusion conceptual framework has some delimitations and barriers that exist; however, the advantages outweigh the disadvantages for peers and students, creating a mainstream setting of integrated classrooms (special classrooms and students with disabilities are integrated into one classroom) (Felder, 2018). Inclusive education is important in all sectors and fields and can help to shape work training, education, and processes such as 508 compliancy as well as other federal government acts and regulations. This theory is important in framing how artificial intelligence can assist with data analysis in management, education, and marketing sectors of training, leadership, research, policy, and development.

Bibliography

Antonopoulou, H., Halkiopoulos, C., Barlou, O., and Beligiannis, G. N. (2021). "Transformational Leadership and Digital Skills in Higher Education Institutes: During the COVID-19 Pandemic." *Emerging Science Journal*, 5(1), 1–15.

Dusin, J., Melanson, A., and Mische-Lawson, L. (2023). "Evidence-Based Practice Models and Frameworks in the Healthcare Setting: A Scoping Review." *BMJ Open*, *13*(5), e071188. https://doi.org/10.1136/bmjopen-2022-071188.

Cochran-Smith, M. (2005). "Teacher Educators as Researchers: Multiple Perspectives." Teaching and teacher education, 21(2), 219–225.

Felder, F. 2018. "The Value of Inclusion." *Journal of Philosophy of Education* 52 (1): 54–70. doi: 10.1111/1467-9752.12280.

Johansson, B., Fogelberg-Dahm, M., and Wadensten, B. (2010). "Evidence-Based Practice: The Importance of Education and Leadership." *Journal of Nursing Management,* 18(1), 70–77.

Khaw, T. Y., Teoh, A. P., Khalid, S. N. A., and Letchmunan, S. (2022). "The Impact of Digital Leadership on Sustainable Performance: A Systematic Literature Review." *Journal of Management Development*, 41(9/10), 514–534.

Sackett, D. L. "Evidence-Based Medicine." *Semin Perinatol,* 1997; 21:3–5. 10.1016/s0146 0005(97)80013-4.

Schuelka, M. J. (2018). "Implementing Inclusive Education."

Reeves, B. R. (2023). *The Impact of Transformational Leadership on Follower Attitudes toward Artificial Intelligence (AI) in the United*

States Air Force (Order No. 30692136). Available from publicly available content database. (2882213698). https://www.proquest.com/ dissertations-theses/impact-transformational-leadership-on follower/ docview/2882213698/se-2.

US Department of Education, Office of Educational Technology, Artificial Intelligence and Future of Teaching and Learning: Insights and Recommendations, Washington, DC, 2023.

Printed in the United States
by Baker & Taylor Publisher Services

Printed in the United States
by Baker & Taylor Publisher Services